# SPANISH-ENGLISH
## Picture Dictionary

### Catherine Bruzzone and Louise Millar

*Illustrations by Louise Comfort and Steph Dix*
*Spanish adviser: Diego Blasco Vázquez*

B.E.S.
PUBLISHING

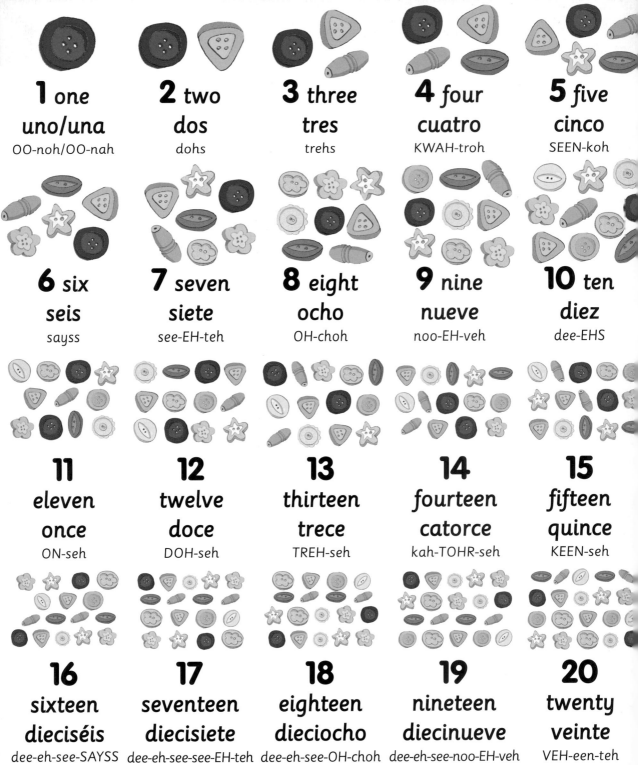

**1** one
uno/una
*OO-noh/OO-nah*

**2** two
dos
*dohs*

**3** three
tres
*trehs*

**4** four
cuatro
*KWAH-troh*

**5** five
cinco
*SEEN-koh*

**6** six
seis
*sayss*

**7** seven
siete
*see-EH-teh*

**8** eight
ocho
*OH-choh*

**9** nine
nueve
*noo-EH-veh*

**10** ten
diez
*dee-EHS*

**11** eleven
once
*ON-seh*

**12** twelve
doce
*DOH-seh*

**13** thirteen
trece
*TREH-seh*

**14** fourteen
catorce
*kah-TOHR-seh*

**15** fifteen
quince
*KEEN-seh*

**16** sixteen
dieciséis
*dee-eh-see-SAYSS*

**17** seventeen
diecisiete
*dee-eh-see-see-EH-teh*

**18** eighteen
dieciocho
*dee-eh-see-OH-choh*

**19** nineteen
diecinueve
*dee-eh-see-noo-EH-veh*

**20** twenty
veinte
*VEH-een-teh*

# Contents – Índice

EEN-dee-seh

# The body – El cuerpo
ehl koo-EHR-poh

**head**
**la cabeza**
lah kah-BEH-sah

**eyes**
**los ojos**
lohs OH-hos

**nose**
**la nariz**
lah nah-REES

**mouth**
**la boca**
lah BOH-kah

**shoulders**
**los hombros**
lohs OHM-brohs

**arm**
**el brazo**
ehl BRAH-soh

**hand**
**la mano**
lah MAH-noh

**leg**
**la pierna**
lah pee-EHR-nah

**foot**
**el pie**
ehl pee-EH

4

# Clothes – La ropa
lah ROH-pah

**skirt**
**la falda**
lah FAHL-dah

**dress**
**el vestido**
ehl vehs-TEE-doh

**pants**
**el pantalón**
ehl pahn-tah-LOHN

**coat**
**el abrigo**
ehl ah-BREE-goh

**shirt**
**la camisa**
lah kah-MEE-sah

**pajamas**
**el pijama**
ehl pee-HAH-mah

**shoes**
**los zapatos**
lohs sah-PAH-tohs

**socks**
**los calcetines**
lohs kahl-see-TEE-nehs

**hat**
**el sombrero**
ehl sohm-BREH-roh

5

# The family – La familia
lah fah-MEE-lee-ah

**mother/Mom**
**la madre/mamá**
*lah MAH-dreh/mah-MAH*

**father/Dad**
**el padre/papá**
*ehl PAH-dreh/pah-PAH*

**sister**
**la hermana**
*lah ehr-MAH-nah*

**brother**
**el hermano**
*ehl ehr-MAH-noh*

**grandmother**
**la abuela**
*lah ah-BWEH-lah*

**grandfather**
**el abuelo**
*ehl ah-BWEH-loh*

**aunt**
**la tía**
*lah TEE-ah*

**uncle**
**el tío**
*ehl TEE-oh*

**cousins**
**los primos**
*lohs PREE-mohs*

# The house – La casa
lah KAH-sah

**kitchen**
**la cocina**
lah koh-SEE-nah

**living room**
**el salón**
ehl sah-LOHN

**bedroom**
**el dormitorio**
ehl-dohr-mee-TOH-ree-oh

**bathroom**
**el cuarto de baño**
l KWAHR-toh deh BAHN-yoh

**toilet**
**el retrete**
ehl reh-TREH-teh

**stairs**
**las escaleras**
lahs ehs-kah-LEH-rahs

**floor**
**el piso**
ehl PEE-soh

**ceiling**
**el techo**
ehl TEH-choh

**garden**
**el jardín**
ehl hahr-DEEN

# In the house – En la casa
### ehn lah KAH-sah

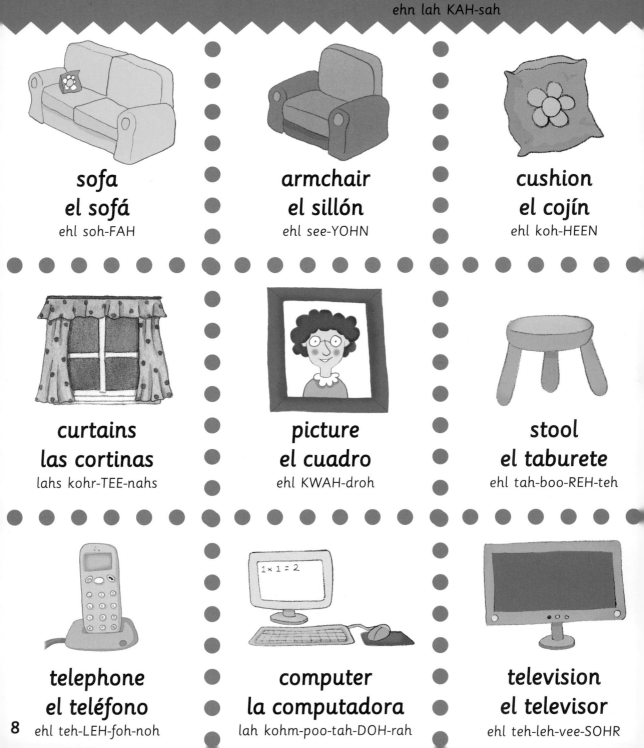

**sofa**
**el sofá**
*ehl soh-FAH*

**armchair**
**el sillón**
*ehl see-YOHN*

**cushion**
**el cojín**
*ehl koh-HEEN*

**curtains**
**las cortinas**
*lahs kohr-TEE-nahs*

**picture**
**el cuadro**
*ehl KWAH-droh*

**stool**
**el taburete**
*ehl tah-boo-REH-teh*

**telephone**
**el teléfono**
*ehl teh-LEH-foh-noh*

**computer**
**la computadora**
*lah kohm-poo-tah-DOH-rah*

**television**
**el televisor**
*ehl teh-leh-vee-SOHR*

# The kitchen – La cocina
lah koh-SEE-nah

**sink**
**el fregadero**
ehl freh-gah-DEH-roh

**refrigerator**
**el refrigerador**
ehl reh-free-heh-rah-DOHR

**stove**
**la cocina**
lah koh-SEE-nah

**knife**
**el cuchillo**
ehl koo-CHEE-yoh

**spoon**
**la cuchara**
lah koo-CHAH-rah

**fork**
**el tenedor**
ehl teh-neh-DOHR

**plate**
**el plato**
ehl PLAH-toh

**glass**
**el vaso**
ehl VAH-soh

**pot**
**la cacerola**
lah kah-seh-ROH-lah

9

# The bedroom – El dormitorio

ehl dohr-mee-TOH-ree-oh

**bed**
**la cama**
lah KAH-mah

**chest of drawers**
**la cómoda**
lah KOH-moh-dah

**wardrobe**
**el armario**
ehl ahr-MAH-ree-oh

**alarm clock**
**el despertador**
ehl dehs-pehr-tah-DOHR

**hairbrush**
**el cepillo del pelo**
ehl seh-PEE-yoh dehl PEH-loh

**shelf**
**el estante**
ehl ehs-TAHN-teh

**rug**
**la alfombra**
10 lah ahl-FOHM-brah

**window**
**la ventana**
lah vehn-TAH-nah

**door**
**la puerta**
lah PWEHR-tah

# The bathroom – El cuarto de baño

ehl KWAHR-toh deh BAHN-yoh

**washbowl**
**el lavamanos**
ehl lah-vah-MAH-nohs

**toilet**
**el retrete**
ehl reh-TREH-teh

**bathtub**
**la bañera**
lah bahn-YEH-rah

**shower**
**la ducha**
lah DOO-chah

**mirror**
**el espejo**
ehl ehs-PEH-hoh

**towel**
**la toalla**
lah toh-AH-yah

**toothpaste**
**la pasta de dientes**
PAHS-tah deh dee-EHN-tehs

**toothbrush**
**el cepillo de dientes**
ehl seh-PEE-yoh deh ee-EHN-tehs

**soap**
**el jabón**
ehl hah-BOHN

11

# The city – La ciudad
lah see-oo-DAHD

**house**
**la casa**
lah KAH-sah

**school**
**la escuela**
lah ehs-KWEH-lah

**station**
**la estación**
lah ehs-tah-see-OHN

**shop**
**la tienda**
lah tee-EHN-dah

**post office**
**la oficina de correos**
lah oh-fee-SEE-nah deh
kohr-REH-ohs

**supermarket**
**el supermercado**
ehl soo-pehr-mehr-KAH-doh

**factory**
**la fábrica**
lah FAH-bree-kah

**market**
**el mercado**
ehl mehr-KAH-doh

**cinema**
**el cine**
ehl SEE-neh

# The street – La calle
### lah KAH-yeh

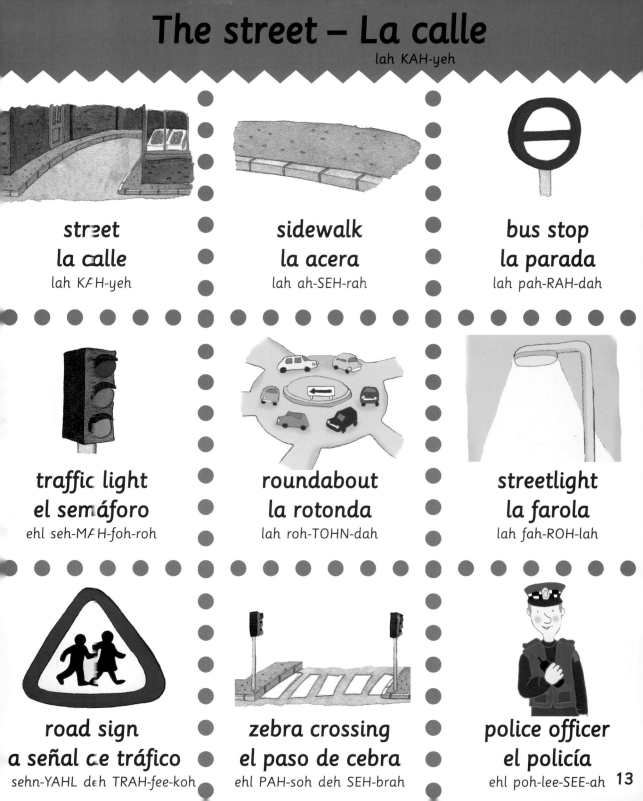

**street**
**la calle**
lah KAH-yeh

**sidewalk**
**la acera**
lah ah-SEH-rah

**bus stop**
**la parada**
lah pah-RAH-dah

**traffic light**
**el semáforo**
ehl seh-MAH-foh-roh

**roundabout**
**la rotonda**
lah roh-TOHN-dah

**streetlight**
**la farola**
lah fah-ROH-lah

**road sign**
**a señal de tráfico**
sehn-YAHL deh TRAH-fee-koh

**zebra crossing**
**el paso de cebra**
ehl PAH-soh deh SEH-brah

**police officer**
**el policía**
ehl poh-lee-SEE-ah

13

# Vehicles – Los vehículos

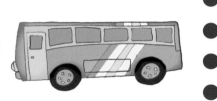

**bus**
**el autobús**
ehl aw-toh-BOOS

**ambulance**
**la ambulancia**
lah ahm-boo-LAHN-see-ah

**bicycle**
**la bicicleta**
lah bee-see-KLEH-tah

**car**
**el coche**
ehl KOH-cheh

**police car**
**el coche de policía**
ehl KOH-cheh deh poh-lee-SEE-ah

**motorcycle**
**la motocicleta**
lah moh-toh-see-KLEH-tah

**truck**
**el camión**
ehl kah-mee-OHN

**fire engine**
**el camión de bomberos**
ehl kah-mee-OHN deh bohm-BEH-rohs

**van**
**la furgoneta**
lah foor-goh-NEH-tah

14

# The park – El parque
ehl PAHR-keh

**path**
**el camino**
ehl kah-MEE-noh

**seesaw**
**el balancín**
ehl bah-lahn-SEEN

**swing**
**el columpio**
ehl koh-LOOM-pee-oh

**girl**
**la niña**
lah NEEN-yah

**boy**
**el niño**
ehl NEEN-yoh

**child**
**el niño/la niña**
ehl NEEN-yoh/lah NEEN-yah

**lake**
**el lago**
ehl LAH-goh

**kite**
**la cometa**
lah koh-MEH-tah

**bench**
**el banco**
ehl BAHN-koh

15

# The hospital – El hospital

ehl ohs-pee-TAHL

**doctor**
**la doctora**
lah dohk-TOH-rah

**nurse**
**el enfermero**
ehl ehn-fehr-MEH-roh

**x-ray**
**la radiografía**
lah rah-dee-oh-grah-FEE-ah

**thermometer**
**el termómetro**
ehl tehr-MOH-meh-troh

**medicine**
**la medicina**
lah meh-dee-SEE-nah

**bandage**
**el vendaje**
ehl vehn-DAH-heh

**cast**
**la escayola**
lah ehs-kah-YOH-lah

**crutches**
**las muletas**
lahs moo-LEH-tahs

**wheelchair**
**la silla de ruedas**
lah SEE-yah deh RWEH-dah

16

# The supermarket – El supermercado

**egg**
**el huevo**
ehl HWEH-voh

**bread**
**el pan**
ehl pahn

**meat**
**la carne**
lah KAHR-neh

**rice**
**el arroz**
ehl ahr-ROHS

**fish**
**el pescado**
ehl pehs-KAH-doh

**butter**
**la mantequilla**
lah mahn-teh-KEE-yah

**milk**
**la leche**
lah LEH-cheh

**pasta**
**la pasta**
lah PAHS-tah

**sugar**
**el azúcar**
ehl ah-SOO-kahr

17

# Fruit – La fruta

lah FROO-tah

**apple**
**la manzana**
lah mahn-SAH-nah

**peach**
**el melocotón**
ehl meh-loh-koh-TOHN

**cherry**
**la cereza**
lah seh-REH-sah

**orange**
**la naranja**
lah nah-RAHN-hah

**pineapple**
**la piña**
lah PEEN-yah

**mango**
**el mango**
ehl MAHN-goh

**banana**
**el plátano**
ehl PLAH-tah-noh

**grapes**
**las uvas**
lahs OO-vahs

**strawberry**
**la fresa**
lah FREH-sah

18

# Vegetables – Las verduras

lahs vehr-DOO-rahs

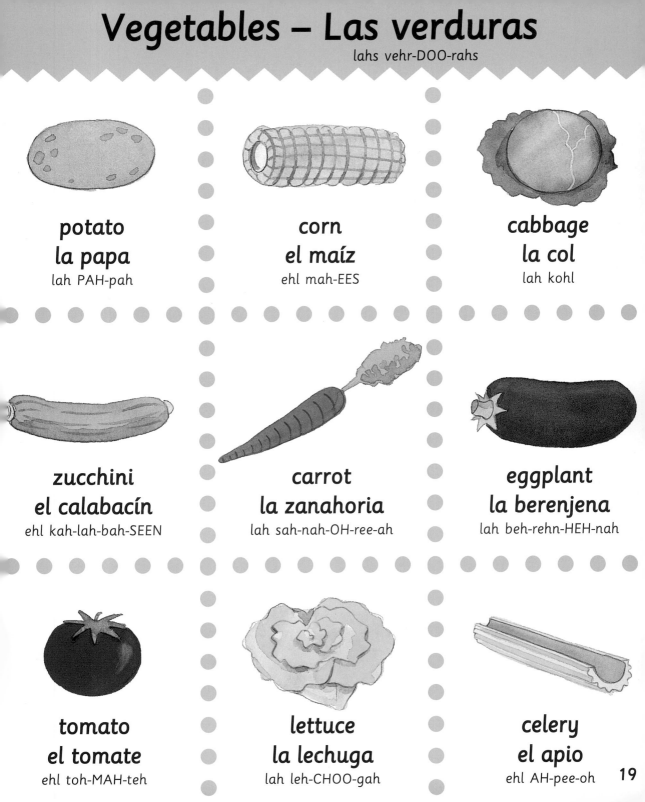

**potato**
**la papa**
lah PAH-pah

**corn**
**el maíz**
ehl mah-EES

**cabbage**
**la col**
lah kohl

**zucchini**
**el calabacín**
ehl kah-lah-bah-SEEN

**carrot**
**la zanahoria**
lah sah-nah-OH-ree-ah

**eggplant**
**la berenjena**
lah beh-rehn-HEH-nah

**tomato**
**el tomate**
ehl toh-MAH-teh

**lettuce**
**la lechuga**
lah leh-CHOO-gah

**celery**
**el apio**
ehl AH-pee-oh

19

**tree**
**el árbol**
ehl AHR-bohl

**grass**
**la hierba**
lah ee-EHR-bah

**flower**
**la flor**
lah flohr

**field**
**el prado**
ehl PRAH-doh

**forest**
**el bosque**
ehl BOHS-keh

**mountain**
**la montaña**
lah mohn-TAHN-yah

**bridge**
**el puente**
ehl PWEHN-teh

**river**
**el río**
ehl REE-oh

**bird**
**el pájaro**
ehl PAH-hah-roh

20

# In the forest – En el bosque

ehn ehl BOHS-keh

**fox**
**el zorro**

ehl SCHR-roh

**squirrel**
**la ardilla**

lah ahr-DEE-yah

**deer**
**el ciervo**

ehl see-EHR-voh

**rabbit**
**el conejo**

ehl koh-NEH-hoh

**brown bear**
**el oso marrón**

ehl OH-soh mahr-ROHN

**butterfly**
**la mariposa**

lah mah-ree-POH-sah

**beetle**
**el escarabajo**

ehl ehs-kah-rah-BAH-hoh

**caterpillar**
**la oruga**

lah oh-ROO-gah

**fly**
**la mosca**

lah MOHS-kah

21

# The farm – La granja

lah GRAHN-hah

**cat**
**el gato**
ehl GAH-toh

**mouse**
**el ratón**
ehl rah-TOHN

**dog**
**el perro**
ehl PEHR-roh

**cow**
**la vaca**
lah VAH-kah

**horse**
**el caballo**
ehl kah-BAH-yoh

**pig**
**el cerdo**
ehl SEHR-doh

**sheep**
**la oveja**
lah oh-VEH-hah

**duck**
**el pato**
ehl PAH-toh

**goat**
**la cabra**
lah KAH-brah

# Baby animals – Las crías de animales
lahs KREE-ahs deh ah-nee-MAH-lehs

**puppy**
**el cachorro**
ehl kah-CHOHR-roh

**kitten**
**el gatito**
ehl gah-TEE-toh

**foal**
**el potro**
ehl POH-troh

**calf**
**el ternero**
ehl tehr-NEH-roh

**chick**
**el pollito**
ehl poh-YEE-toh

**cygnet**
**el pichón de cisne**
ehl pee-CHOHN deh SEES-neh

**duckling**
**el patito**
ehl pah-TEE-toh

**lamb**
**el cordero**
ehl kohr-DEH-roh

**piglet**
**el cerdito**
ehl sehr-DEE-toh

23

# At the beach – En la playa

ehn lah PLAH-yah

**sea**
**el mar**
ehl mahr

**seagull**
**la gaviota**
lah gah-vee-OH-tah

**sand**
**la arena**
lah ah-REH-nah

**fish**
**el pez**
ehl pehs

**seaweed**
**el alga marina**
ehl AHL-gah mah-REE-nah

**shell**
**la concha**
lah KOHN-chah

**rock**
**la roca**
lah ROH-kah

**sailboat**
**el velero**
ehl veh-LEH-roh

**wave**
**la ola**
lah OH-lah

24

# Under the sea – Bajo el mar

BAH-oh ehl mahr

**octopus**
**el pulpo**
ehl POOL-poh

**starfish**
**la estrella de mar**
lah ehs-TREH-yah deh mahr

**jellyfish**
**la medusa**
lah meh-DOO-sah

**lobster**
**la langosta**
lah lahn-GOHS-tah

**shark**
**el tiburón**
ehl tee-boo-ROHN

**whale**
**la ballena**
lah bah-YEH-nah

**wreck**
**el naufragio**
ehl nah-oo-FRAH-hee-oh

**diver**
**el buceador**
ehl boo-seh-ah-DOHR

**coral**
**el coral**
ehl koh-RAHL

25

# The zoo – El zoológico

ehl soh-oh-LOH-hee-koh

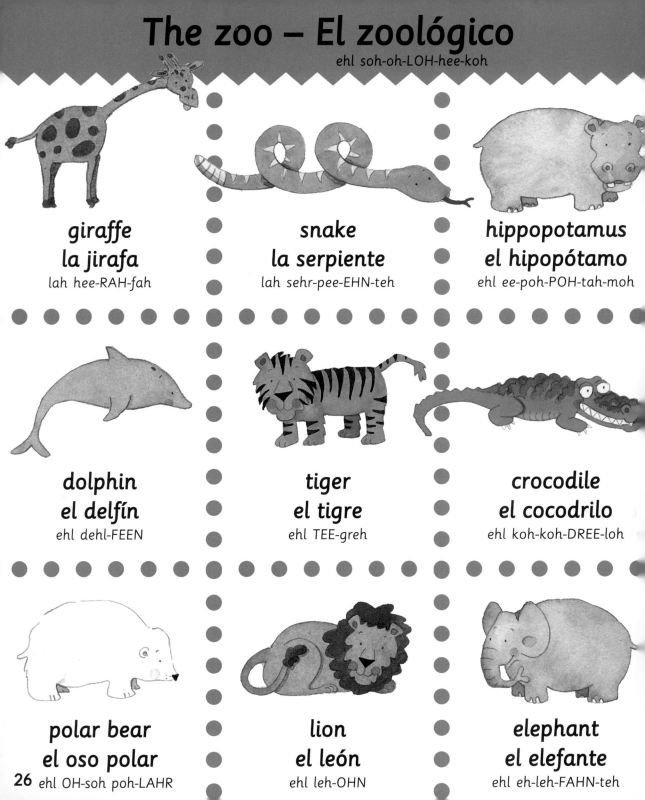

**giraffe**
**la jirafa**
lah hee-RAH-fah

**snake**
**la serpiente**
lah sehr-pee-EHN-teh

**hippopotamus**
**el hipopótamo**
ehl ee-poh-POH-tah-moh

**dolphin**
**el delfín**
ehl dehl-FEEN

**tiger**
**el tigre**
ehl TEE-greh

**crocodile**
**el cocodrilo**
ehl koh-koh-DREE-loh

**polar bear**
**el oso polar**
**26** ehl OH-soh poh-LAHR

**lion**
**el león**
ehl leh-OHN

**elephant**
**el elefante**
ehl eh-leh-FAHN-teh

# Toys – Los juguetes

los hoo-GEH-tehs

**teddy bear**
**el osito**
ehl oh-SEE-toh

**robot**
**el robot**
ehl roh-BOHT

**ball**
**la pelota**
lah peh-LOH-tah

**puzzle**
**el rompecabezas**
ehl rohm-peh-kah-BEH-sahs

**toy train**
**el trencito de juguete**
ehl trehn-SEE-toh deh hoo-GEH-teh

**game**
**el juego**
ehl HWEH-goh

**doll**
**la muñeca**
lah moon-YEH-kah

**paints**
**las pinturas**
lahs peen-TOO-rahs

**drum**
**el tambor**
ehl tahm-BOHR

27

# Party time! – ¡Fiesta!
fee-EHS-tah

**sandwich**
**el bocadillo**
ehl boh-kah-DEE-yoh

**chocolate**
**el chocolate**
ehl choh-koh-LAH-teh

**french fries**
**las papas fritas**
lahs PAH-pahs FREE-tahs

**pizza**
**la pizza**
lah PEE-tsah

**cake**
**la torta**
lah TOHR-tah

**ice cream**
**el helado**
ehl eh-LAH-doh

**cola**
**el refresco**
ehl reh-FREHS-koh

**orange juice**
**el jugo de naranja**
ehl HOO-goh deh nah-RAHN-hah

**water**
**el agua**
ehl AH-gwah

28

# The classroom – La clase
lah KLAH-seh

**teacher**
**la profesora**
lah proh-feh-SOH-rah

**table**
**la mesa**
lah MEH-sah

**chair**
**la silla**
lah SEE-yah

**book**
**el libro**
ehl LEE-broh

**color pencil**
**el lápiz de color**
ehl LAH-pees deh koh-LOHR

**glue**
**el pegamento**
ehl peh-gah-MEHN-toh

**paper**
**el papel**
ehl pah-PEHL

**pen**
**la pluma**
lah PLOO-mah

**scissors**
**las tijeras**
lahs tee-HEH-rahs

# Sports - Los deportes

**soccer**
**el fútbol**
ehl FOOT-bohl

**table tennis**
**el ping pong**
ehl peeng pohng

**skiing**
**el esquí**
ehl ehs-KEY

**gymnastics**
**la gimnasia**
lah heem-NAH-see-ah

**cycling**
**el ciclismo**
ehl see-KLEES-moh

**athletics**
**el atletismo**
ehl aht-leh-TEES-moh

**fishing**
**la pesca**
lah PEHS-kah

**swimming**
**la natación**
lah nah-tah-see-OHN

**basketball**
**el baloncesto**
ehl bah-lohn-SEHS-toh

30

# Weather – El tiempo
ehl tee-EHM-poh

**sun**
**el sol**
ehl sohl

**heat**
**el calor**
ehl kah-LOHR

**rain**
**la lluvia**
lah YOO-vee-ah

**cloud**
**la nube**
lah NOO-beh

**wind**
**el viento**
ehl vee-EHN-toh

**storm**
**la tormenta**
lah tohr-MEHN-tah

*fog*
*la niebla*
lah nee-EH-blah

**cold**
**el frío**
ehl FREE-oh

**snow**
**la nieve**
lah nee-EH-veh

31

# Action words – Palabras de acción

pah-LAH-brahs deh ahk-see-OHN

**to run**
**correr**
kohr-REHR

**to walk**
**andar**
ahn-DAHR

**to crawl**
**gatear**
gah-teh-AHR

**to carry**
**llevar**
yeh-VAHR

**to stand**
**estar de pie**
ehs-TAHR deh pee-EH

**to sit**
**estar sentado**
ehs-TAHR sehn-TAH-doh

**to push**
**empujar**
ehm-poo-HAHR

**to hug**
**abrazar**
ah-brah-SAHR

**to pull**
**halar**
hah-LAHR

# Storybooks – Los libros de cuentos

**dragon**
**el dragón**
ehl drah-GOHN

**mermaid**
**la sirena**
lah see-REH-nah

**knight**
**el caballero**
ehl kah-bah-YEH-roh

**pirate**
**el pirata**
ehl pee-RAH-tah

**fairy**
**el hada**
ehl AH-dah

**witch**
**la bruja**
lah BROO-hah

**prince**
**el príncipe**
ehl PREEN-see-peh

**princess**
**la princesa**
lah preen-SEH-sah

**castle**
**el castillo**
ehl kahs-TEE-yoh

33

# The building site – La obra

**digger**
**la excavadora**
lah ex-kah-vah-DOH-rah

**cement mixer**
**el camión hormigonera**
ehl kah-mee-OHN
ohr-mee-goh-NEH-rah

**crane**
**la grúa**
lah GROO-ah

**scaffolding**
**el andamio**
ehl ahn-DAH-mee-oh

**dump truck**
**el camión volquete**
ehl kah-mee-OHN vohl-KEH-teh

**brick**
**el ladrillo**
ehl lah-DREE-yoh

**bulldozer**
**el bulldozer**
ehl bool-DOH-zehr

**ladder**
**la escalera**
lah ehs-kah-LEH-rah

**wood**
**el tablón**
ehl tah-BLOHN

34

# Tools – Las herramientas

lahs ehr-rah-mee-EHN-tahs

**rake**
**el rastrillo**
ehl rahs-TREE-yoh

**shovel**
**la pala**
lah PAH-lah

**bucket**
**el cubo**
ehl KOO-boh

**wheelbarrow**
**la carretilla**
lah kahr-reh-TEE-yah

**hammer**
**el martillo**
ehl mahr-TEE-yoh

**nail**
**el clavo**
ehl KLAH-voh

**saw**
**el serrucho**
ehl sehr-ROO-choh

**hose**
**la manguera**
lah mahn-GEH-rah

**paintbrush**
**la brocha**
lah BROH-chah

35

# Luggage – El equipaje
ehl eh-kee-PAH-heh

**suitcase**
**la maleta**
lah mah-LEH-tah

**schoolbag**
**el bolsón**
ehl bohl-SOHN

**trunk**
**el baúl**
ehl bah-OOL

**backpack**
**la mochila**
lah moh-CHEE-lah

**handbag**
**la cartera**
lah kahr-TEH-rah

**briefcase**
**el maletín**
ehl mah-leh-TEEN

**basket**
**la cesta**
lah SEHS-tah

**shopping bag**
**la bolsa de compras**
lah BOHL-sah deh KOHM-prahs

**purse**
**el monedero**
ehl moh-neh-DEH-roh

36

# Train travel – El viaje en tren

ehl vee-AH-heh ehn trehn

**ticket**
**el billete**
ehl bee-YEH-teh

**conductor**
**el revisor**
ehl reh-vee-SOHR

**platform**
**el andén**
ehl ahn-DEHN

**engineer**
**la maquinista**
lah mah-kee-NEES-tah

**signal**
**la señal**
lah sehn-YAHL

**train**
**el tren**
ehl trehn

**seat**
**el asiento**
ehl ah-see-EHN-toh

**level crossing**
**el paso a nivel**
ehl PAH-soh ah nee-VEHL

**rails**
**los rieles**
lohs ree-EH-lehs

37

# Air travel – El viaje en avión

ehl vee-AH-heh ehn ah-vee-OHN

**airplane**
**el avión**
ehl ah-vee-OHN

**airport**
**el aeropuerto**
ehl ah-eh-roh-PWEHR-toh

**pilot**
**el piloto**
ehl pee-LOH-toh

**flight attendant**
**la azafata**
lah ah-sah-FAH-tah

**x-ray machine**
**la máquina de rayos x**
lah MAH-kee-nah
deh RAH-yohs EH-kees

**passport**
**el pasaporte**
ehl pah-sah-POHR-teh

**hand truck**
**el carrito**
ehl kahr-REE-toh

**snack**
**el refrigerio**
ehl reh-free-HEH-ree-oh

**seatbelt**
**el cinturón de segurid**
ehl seen-too-ROHN deh
seh-goo-ree-DAHD

38

# At sea – En el mar
### ehn ehl mahr

**sh.p**
**el barco**
ehl BAHR-koh

**yacht**
**el yate**
ehl YAH-teh

**rowboat**
**el bote a remos**
ehl BOH-teh ah REH-mohs

**tanker**
**el petrolero**
ehl peh-troh-LEH-roh

**fishing boat**
**el barco de pesca**
ehl BAHR-koh deh PEHS-kah

**ferry**
**el ferry**
ehl FEHR-ree

**buoy**
**la boya**
lay 3OH-yah

**port**
**el puerto**
ehl PWEHR-toh

**lighthouse**
**el faro**
ehl FAH-roh

# Opposites – Los contrarios

lohs kohn-TRAH-ree-ohs

**friendly**
**amable**
ah-MAH-bleh

**angry**
**enojado/enojada**
eh-noh-HAH-doh/eh-noh-HAH-dah

**thin**
**delgado/delgada**
dehl-GAH-doh/dehl-GAH-dah

**clean**
**limpio/limpia**
LEEM-pee-oh/LEEM-pee-ah

**dirty**
**sucio/sucia**
SOO-see-oh/SOO-see-ah

**neat**
**ordenado/ordenada**
ohr-deh-NAH-doh/ohr-deh-NAH-

**sad**
**triste**
TREES-teh

**happy**
**feliz**
feh-LEES

**heavy**
**pesado/pesada**
peh-SAH-doh/peh-SAH-dah

# Opposites – Los contrarios
lohs kohn-TRAH-ree-ohs

**fat**
**gordo/gorda**
GOHR-doh/GOHR-dah

**tall**
**alto/alta**
AHL-toh/AHL-tah

**short**
**bajo/baja**
BAH-hoh/BAH-hah

**messy**
**desordenado/desordenada**
deh-sohr-deh-NAH-doh/
deh-sohr-deh-NAH-dah

**fast**
**rápido/rápida**
RAH-pee-doh/RAH-pee-dah

**slow**
**lento/lenta**
LEHN-toh/LEHN-tah

**light**
**ligero/ligera**
lee-HEH-roh/lee-HEH-rah

**beautiful**
**hermoso/hermosa**
ehr-MOH-soh/ehr-MOH-sah

**ugly**
**feo/fea**
FEH-oh/FEH-ah

41

# Spanish/español – English/inglés

abrazar  to hug
el abrigo  coat
la abuela  grandmother
el abuelo  grandfather
la acera  sidewalk
el aeropuerto  airport
el agua  water
la alfombra  rug
el alga marina  seaweed
alto/alta  tall
amable  friendly
amarillo/amarilla  yellow
la ambulancia  ambulance
el andamio  scaffolding
andar  to walk
el andén  platform
el apio  celery
el árbol  tree
la ardilla  squirrel
la arena  sand
el armario  wardrobe
el arroz  rice
el asiento  seat
el atletismo  athletics
el autobús  bus
el avión  airplane
la azafata  flight attendant
el azúcar  sugar
azul  blue
bajo/baja  short
el balancín  seesaw
la ballena  whale
el baloncesto  basketball
el banco  bench
la bañera  bathtub
el barco  ship
el barco de pesca  fishing boat
el baúl  trunk
la berenjena  eggplant
la bicicleta  bicycle
el billete  ticket

blanco/blanca  white
la boca  mouth
el bocadillo  sandwich
la bolsa de compras  shopping bag
el bolsón  schoolbag
el bosque  forest
el bote a remos  rowboat
la boya  buoy
el brazo  arm
la brocha  paintbrush
la bruja  witch
el buceador  diver
el bulldozer  bulldozer
el caballero  knight
el caballo  horse
la cabeza  head
la cabra  goat
la cacerola  pot
el cachorro  puppy
el calabacín  zucchini
los calcetines  socks
la calle  street
el calor  heat
la cama  bed
el camino  path
el camión  truck
el camión de bomberos  fire engine
el camión hormigonera
    cement mixer
el camión volquete  dump truck
la camisa  shirt
el campo  country
la carne  meat
la carretilla  wheelbarrow
la cartera  handbag
el carrito  hand truck
la casa  house
el castillo  castle
catorce  fourteen
el cepillo de dientes  toothbrush
el cepillo del pelo  hairbrush
el cerdito  piglet

el cerdo  pig
la cereza  cherry
la cesta  basket
el chocolate  chocolate
el ciclismo  cycling
el ciervo  deer
cinco  five
el cine  cinema
el cinturón de seguridad  seatbelt
la ciudad  city
la clase  classroom
el clavo  nail
el coche  car
el coche de policía  police car
la cocina  kitchen, stove
el cocodrilo  crocodile
el cojín  cushion
la col  cabbage
los colores  colors
la cometa  kite
la cómoda  chest of drawers
la computadora  computer
la concha  shell
el conejo  rabbit
el coral  coral
el cordero  lamb
correr  to run
las cortinas  curtains
el cuadro  picture
el cuarto de baño  bathroom
cuatro  four
el cubo  bucket
la cuchara  spoon
el cuchillo  knife
el cuerpo  body
el delfín  dolphin
delgado/delgada  thin
los deportes  sports
desordenado/desordenada  messy
el despertador  alarm clock
diecinueve  nineteen
dieciocho  eighteen

42

| | | |
|---|---|---|
| **dieciséis** sixteen | **el gato** cat | **la mantequilla** butter |
| **diecisiete** seventeen | **la gaviota** seagull | **la manzana** apple |
| **diez** ten | **la gimnasia** gymnastics | **la máquina de rayos x** x-ray machine |
| **doce** twelve | **gordo/gorda** fat | |
| **la doctora** doctor | **la granja** farm | **la maquinista** engineer |
| **el dormitorio** bedroom | **la grúa** crane | **el mar** sea |
| **dos** two | **el hada** fairy | **la mariposa** butterfly |
| **el dragón** dragon | **halar** to pull | **marrón** brown |
| **la ducha** shower | **el helado** ice cream | **el martillo** hammer |
| **el elefante** elephant | **la hermana** sister | **la matación** swimming |
| **empujar** to push | **el hermano** brother | **la medicina** medicine |
| **el enfermero** nurse | **hermoso/hermosa** beautiful | **la medusa** jellyfish |
| **enojado/enojada** angry | **las herramientas** tools | **el melocotón** peach |
| **el equipaje** luggage | **la hierba** grass | **el mercado** market |
| **la escalera** ladder | **el hipopótamo** hippopotamus | **la mesa** table |
| **las escaleras** stairs | **los hombros** shoulders | **la mochila** backpack |
| **el escarabajo** beetle | **el hospital** hospital | **el monedero** purse |
| **la escayola** cast | **el huevo** egg | **la montaña** mountain |
| **la escuela** school | **el jabón** soap | **morado/morada** purple |
| **el espejo** mirror | **el jardín** garden | **la mosca** fly |
| **el esquí** skiing | **la jirafa** giraffe | **la motocicleta** motorcycle |
| **la estación** station | **el jugo de naranja** orange juice | **las muletas** crutches |
| **el estante** shelf | **el juguete** toy | **la muñeca** doll |
| **estar de pie** to stand | **el ladrillo** brick | **la naranja** orange (fruit) |
| **estar sentado** to sit | **el lago** lake | **naranja** orange (color) |
| **la estrella de mar** starfish | **la langosta** lobster | **la nariz** nose |
| **la excavadora** digger | **el lápiz de color** color pencil | **la natación** swimming |
| **la fábrica** factory | **el lavamanos** washbowl | **el naufragio** wreck |
| **la falda** skirt | **la leche** milk | **negro/negra** black |
| **la familia** family | **la lechuga** lettuce | **la niebla** fog |
| **el faro** lighthouse | **lento/lenta** slow | **la nieve** snow |
| **la farola** streetlight | **el león** lion | **la niña** girl |
| **feliz** happy | **el libro** book | **el niño** boy |
| **feo/fea** ugly | **ligero/ligera** light | **el niño/la niña** child |
| **el ferry** ferry | **limpio/limpia** clean | **la nube** cloud |
| **la fiesta** party | **llevar** to carry | **nueve** nine |
| **la flor** flower | **la lluvia** rain | **la obra** building site |
| **el fregadero** sink | **la madre** mother | **ocho** eight |
| **la fresa** strawberry | **el maíz** corn | **la oficina de correos** post office |
| **el frío** cold | **la maleta** suitcase | **los ojos** eyes |
| **la fruta** fruit | **el maletín** briefcase | **la ola** wave |
| **la furgoneta** van | **mamá** Mom | **once** eleven |
| **el fútbol** soccer | **el mango** mango | **ordenado/ordenada** neat |
| **gatear** to crawl | **la manguera** hose | **la oruga** caterpillar |
| **el gatito** kitten | **la mano** hand | **el osito** teddy bear |

|  |  |  |  |  |  |
|---|---|---|---|---|---|
| **el oso marrón** | brown bear | **el pollito** | chick | **el supermercado** | supermarket |
| **el oso polar** | polar bear | **el potro** | foal | **el tablón** | wood |
| **la oveja** | sheep | **el prado** | field | **el taburete** | stool |
| **el padre** | father | **los primos** | cousins | **el tambor** | drum |
| **el pájaro** | bird | **la princesa** | princess | **el techo** | ceiling |
| **la pala** | shovel | **el príncipe** | prince | **el teléfono** | telephone |
| **el pan** | bread | **la profesora** | teacher | **el televisor** | television |
| **el pantalón** | pants | **el puente** | bridge | **el tenedor** | fork |
| **papá** | Dad | **la puerta** | door | **el termómetro** | thermometer |
| **la papa** | potato | **el puerto** | port | **el ternero** | calf |
| **las papas fritas** | french fries | **el pulpo** | octopus | **la tía** | aunt |
| **el papel** | paper | **quince** | fifteen | **el tiburón** | shark |
| **la parada** | bus stop | **la radiografía** | x-ray | **el tiempo** | weather |
| **el pasaporte** | passport | **rápido/rápida** | fast | **la tienda** | shop |
| **el paso a nivel** | level crossing | **el rastrillo** | rake | **el tigre** | tiger |
| **el paso de cebra** | zebra crossing | **el ratón** | mouse | **las tijeras** | scissors |
| **la pasta** | pasta | **el refresco** | cola | **el tío** | uncle |
| **la pasta de dientes** | toothpaste | **el refrigerador** | refrigerator | **la toalla** | towel |
| **el patito** | duckling | **el refrigerio** | snack | **el tomate** | tomato |
| **el pato** | duck | **el retrete** | toilet | **la tormenta** | storm |
| **el pegamento** | glue | **el revisor** | conductor | **la torta** | cake |
| **la pelota** | ball | **los rieles** | rails | **trece** | thirteen |
| **el perro** | dog | **el río** | river | **el tren** | train |
| **pesado/pesada** | heavy | **el robot** | robot | **el trencito de juguete** | toy train |
| **el pescado** | fish (to eat) | **la roca** | rock | **tres** | three |
| **la pesca** | fishing | **rojo/roja** | red | **triste** | sad |
| **el petrolero** | tanker | **el rompecabezas** | puzzle | **uno/una** | one |
| **el pez** | fish (in the sea) | **la ropa** | clothes | **las uvas** | grapes |
| **el pichón de cisne** | cygnet | **la rotonda** | roundabout | **la vaca** | cow |
| **el pie** | foot | **el salón** | living room | **el vaso** | glass |
| **la pierna** | leg | **seis** | six | **los vehículos** | vehicles |
| **el pijama** | pajamas | **el semáforo** | traffic light | **veinte** | twenty |
| **el piloto** | pilot | **la señal** | signal | **el velero** | sailboat |
| **la piña** | pineapple | **la señal de tráfico** | road sign | **el vendaje** | bandage |
| **el ping pong** | table tennis | **la serpiente** | snake | **la ventana** | window |
| **las pinturas** | paints | **el serrucho** | saw | **verde** | green |
| **el pirata** | pirate | **siete** | seven | **las verduras** | vegetables |
| **el piso** | floor | **la silla** | chair | **el vestido** | dress |
| **la pizza** | pizza | **la silla de ruedas** | wheelchair | **el viaje** | travel |
| **el plátano** | banana | **el sillón** | armchair | **el viento** | wind |
| **el plato** | plate | **la sirena** | mermaid | **el yate** | yacht |
| **la playa** | beach | **el sofá** | sofa | **la zanahoria** | carrot |
| **la pluma** | pen | **el sol** | sun | **los zapatos** | shoes |
| **el policía** | police officer | **el sombrero** | hat | **el zoológico** | zoo |
| | | **sucio/sucia** | dirty | **el zorro** | fox |

# English/inglés – Spanish/español

**airplane**  el avión
**airport**  el aeropuerto
**alarm clock**  el despertador
**ambulance**  la ambulancia
**angry**  enojado/enojada
**apple**  la manzana
**arm**  el brazo
**armchair**  el sillón
**athletics**  el atletismo
**aunt**  la tía
**backpack**  la mochila
**ball**  la pelota
**banana**  el plátano
**bandage**  el vendaje
**basket**  la cesta
**basketball**  el baloncesto
**bathroom**  el cuarto de baño
**bathtub**  la bañera
**beach**  la playa
**beautiful**  hermoso/hermosa
**bed**  la cama
**bedroom**  el dormitorio
**beetle**  el escarabajo
**bench**  el banco
**bicycle**  la bicicleta
**bird**  el pájaro
**black**  negro/negra
**blue**  azul
**body**  el cuerpo
**book**  el libro
**boy**  el niño
**bread**  el pan
**brick**  el ladrillo
**bridge**  el puente
**briefcase**  el maletín
**brother**  el hermano
**brown**  marrón
**brown bear**  el oso marrón
**bucket**  el cubo
**building site**  la obra
**bulldozer**  el buldózer
**buoy**  la boya

**bus**  el autobús
**bus stop**  la parada
**butter**  la mantequilla
**butterfly**  la mariposa
**cabbage**  la col
**cake**  la torta
**calf**  el ternero
**car**  el coche
**carrot**  la zanahoria
**to carry**  llevar
**cast**  la escayola
**castle**  el castillo
**cat**  el gato
**caterpillar**  la oruga
**ceiling**  el techo
**celery**  el apio
**cement mixer**
   el camión hormigonera
**chair**  la silla
**cherry**  la cereza
**chest of drawers**  la cómoda
**chick**  el pollito
**child**  el niño/la niña
**chocolate**  el chocolate
**cinema**  el cine
**city**  la ciudad
**classroom**  la clase
**clean**  limpio/limpia
**clothes**  la ropa
**cloud**  la nube
**coat**  el abrigo
**cola**  el refresco
**cold**  el frío
**color pencil**  el lápiz de color
**colors**  los colores
**computer**  la computadora
**conductor**  el revisor
**coral**  el coral
**corn**  el maíz
**country**  el campo
**cousins**  los primos
**cow**  la vaca

**crane**  la grúa
**to crawl**  gatear
**crocodile**  el cocodrilo
**crutches**  las muletas
**curtains**  las cortinas
**cushion**  el cojín
**cycling**  ciclismo
**cygnet**  el pichón de cisne
**Dad**  papá
**deer**  el ciervo
**digger**  la excavadora
**dirty**  sucio/sucia
**diver**  el buceador
**doctor**  la doctora
**dog**  el perro
**doll**  la muñeca
**dolphin**  el delfín
**door**  la puerta
**dragon**  el dragón
**dress**  el vestido
**drum**  el tambor
**duck**  el pato
**duckling**  el patito
**dump truck**  el camión volquete
**egg**  el huevo
**eggplant**  la berenjena
**eight**  ocho
**eighteen**  dieciocho
**elephant**  el elefante
**eleven**  once
**engineer**  la maquinista
**eyes**  los ojos
**factory**  la fábrica
**fairy**  el hada
**family**  la familia
**farm**  la granja
**fast**  rápido/rápida
**fat**  gordo/gorda
**father**  el padre
**ferry**  el ferry
**field**  el prado
**fifteen**  quince

| | | |
|---|---|---|
| **fire engine** el camión de bomberos | **horse** el caballo | **one** uno/una |
| **fish (to eat)** el pescado | **hose** la manguera | **orange (fruit)** la naranja |
| **fish (in the sea)** el pez | **hospital** el hospital | **orange (color)** naranja |
| **fishing** la pesca | **house** la casa | **orange juice** el jugo de naranja |
| **fishing boat** el barco de pesca | **to hug** abrazar | **paintbrush** la brocha |
| **five** cinco | **ice cream** el helado | **paints** las pinturas |
| **flight attendant** la azafata | **jellyfish** la medusa | **pajamas** el pijama |
| **floor** el piso | **kitchen** la cocina | **pants** el pantalón |
| **flower** la flor | **kite** la cometa | **paper** el papel |
| **fly** la mosca | **kitten** el gatito | **party** la fiesta |
| **foal** el potro | **knife** el cuchillo | **passport** el pasaporte |
| **fog** la niebla | **knight** el caballero | **pasta** la pasta |
| **foot** el pie | **ladder** la escalera | **path** el camino |
| **forest** el bosque | **lake** el lago | **peach** el melocotón |
| **fork** el tenedor | **lamb** el cordero | **pen** la pluma |
| **four** cuatro | **leg** la pierna | **picture** el cuadro |
| **fourteen** catorce | **lettuce** la lechuga | **pig** el cerdo |
| **fox** el zorro | **level crossing** el paso a nivel | **piglet** el cerdito |
| **french fries** las papas fritas | **light** ligero/ligera | **pilot** el piloto |
| **friendly** amable | **lighthouse** el faro | **pineapple** la piña |
| **fruit** la fruta | **lion** el león | **pirate** el pirata |
| **garden** el jardín | **living room** el salón | **pizza** la pizza |
| **giraffe** la jirafa | **lobster** la langosta | **plate** el plato |
| **girl** la niña | **luggage** el equipaje | **platform** el andén |
| **glass** el vaso | **mango** el mango | **polar bear** el oso polar |
| **glue** el pegamento | **market** el mercado | **police car** el coche de policía |
| **goat** la cabra | **meat** la carne | **police officer** el policía |
| **grandfather** el abuelo | **medicine** la medicina | **port** el puerto |
| **grandmother** la abuela | **mermaid** la sirena | **post office** la oficina de correos |
| **grapes** las uvas | **messy** desordenado/desordenada | **pot** la cacerola |
| **grass** la hierba | **milk** la leche | **potato** la papa |
| **green** verde | **mirror** el espejo | **prince** el príncipe |
| **gymnastics** la gimnasia | **Mom** mamá | **princess** la princesa |
| **hairbrush** el cepillo del pelo | **mother** la madre | **to pull** halar |
| **hammer** el martillo | **motorcycle** la motocicleta | **puppy** el cachorro |
| **hand** la mano | **mountain** la montaña | **purple** morado/morada |
| **handbag** la cartera | **mouse** el ratón | **purse** el monedero |
| **hand truck** el carrito | **mouth** la boca | **to push** empujar |
| **happy** feliz | **nail** el clavo | **puzzle** el rompecabezas |
| **hat** el sombrero | **neat** ordenado/ordenada | **rabbit** el conejo |
| **head** la cabeza | **nine** nueve | **rails** los rieles |
| **heat** el calor | **nineteen** diecinueve | **rain** la lluvia |
| **heavy** pesado/pesada | **nose** la nariz | **rake** el rastrillo |
| **hippopotamus** el hipopótamo | **nurse** el enfermero | **red** rojo/roja |
| | **octopus** el pulpo | **refrigerator** el refrigerador |

|  |  |
|---|---|
| **rice** el arroz | **sixteen** dieciséis | **tomato** el tomate |
| **river** el río | **skiing** el esquí | **tools** las herramientas |
| **road sign** la señal de tráfico | **skirt** la falda | **toothbrush** el cepillo de dientes |
| **robot** el robot | **slow** lento/lenta | **toothpaste** la pasta de dientes |
| **rock** la roca | **snack** el refrigerio | **towel** la toalla |
| **roundabout** la rotonda | **snake** la serpiente | **toy** el juguete |
| **rowboat** el bote a remos | **snow** la nieve | **toy train** el trencito de juguete |
| **rug** la alfombra | **soap** el jabón | **traffic light** el semáforo |
| **to run** correr | **soccer** el fútbol | **train** el tren |
| **sad** triste | **socks** los calcetines | **travel** el viaje |
| **sailboat** el velero | **sofa** el sofá | **tree** el árbol |
| **sand** la arena | **spoon** la cuchara | **truck** el camión |
| **sandwich** el bocadillo | **sports** los deportes | **trunk** el baúl |
| **saw** el serrucho | **squirrel** la ardilla | **twelve** doce |
| **scaffolding** el andamio | **stairs** las escaleras | **twenty** veinte |
| **school** la escuela | **to stand** estar de pie | **two** dos |
| **schoolbag** el bolsón | **starfish** la estrella de mar | **ugly** feo/fea |
| **scissors** las tijeras | **station** la estación | **uncle** el tío |
| **sea** el mar | **stool** el taburete | **van** la furgoneta |
| **seagull** la gaviota | **storm** la tormenta | **vegetables** las verduras |
| **seat** el asiento | **stove** la cocina | **vehicles** los vehículos |
| **seatbelt** el cinturón de seguridad | **strawberry** la fresa | **to walk** andar |
| **seaweed** el alga marina | **street** la calle | **wardrobe** el armario |
| **seesaw** el balancín | **streetlight** la farola | **washbowl** el lavabo |
| **seven** siete | **sugar** el azúcar | **water** el agua |
| **seventeen** diecisiete | **suitcase** la maleta | **wave** la ola |
| **shark** el tiburón | **sun** el sol | **weather** el tiempo |
| **sheep** la oveja | **supermarket** el supermercado | **whale** la ballena |
| **shelf** el estante | **swimming** la natación | **wheelbarrow** la carretilla |
| **shell** la concha | **table** la mesa | **wheelchair** la silla de ruedas |
| **ship** el barco | **table tennis** el ping pong | **white** blanco/blanca |
| **shirt** la camisa | **tall** alto/alta | **wind** el viento |
| **shoes** los zapatos | **tanker** el petrolero | **window** la ventana |
| **shop** la tienda | **teacher** la profesora | **witch** la bruja |
| **shopping bag** la bolsa de compras | **teddy bear** el osito | **wood** el tablón |
| **short** bajo/baja | **telephone** el teléfono | **wreck** el naufragio |
| **shoulders** los hombros | **television** el televisor | **x-ray** la radiografía |
| **shovel** la pala | **ten** diez | **x-ray machine** |
| **shower** la ducha | **thermometer** el termómetro | la máquina de rayos x |
| **sidewalk** la acera | **thin** delgado/delgada | **yacht** el yate |
| **signal** la señal | **thirteen** trece | **yellow** amarillo/amarilla |
| **sink** el fregadero | **three** tres | **zebra crossing** el paso de cebra |
| **sister** la hermana | **ticket** el billete | **zoo** el zoológico |
| **to sit** estar sentado | **tiger** el tigre | **zucchini** el calabacín |
| **six** seis | **toilet** el retrete | |

# Colors – Los colores

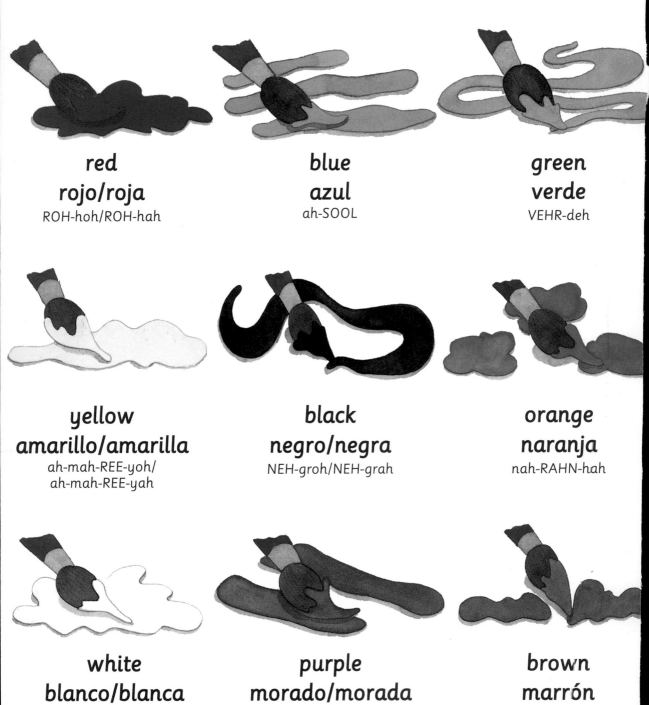

**red**
**rojo/roja**
ROH-hoh/ROH-hah

**blue**
**azul**
ah-SOOL

**green**
**verde**
VEHR-deh

**yellow**
**amarillo/amarilla**
ah-mah-REE-yoh/
ah-mah-REE-yah

**black**
**negro/negra**
NEH-groh/NEH-grah

**orange**
**naranja**
nah-RAHN-hah

**white**
**blanco/blanca**
BLAHN-koh/BLAHN-kah

**purple**
**morado/morada**
moh-RAH-doh/moh-RAH-dah

**brown**
**marrón**
mahr-ROHN